NOW. HERE. THIS.

VINEYARD THEATRE

DOUGLAS AIBEL
ARTISTIC DIRECTOR

JENNIFER GARVEY-BLACKWELL
EXECUTIVE DIRECTOR

SARAH STERN
CO-ARTISTIC DIRECTOR

MANAGING DIRECTOR

PRESENTS

BOOK BY

HUNTER BELL & SUSAN BLACKWELL

MUSIC & LYRICS BY

JEFF BOWEN

BASED ON A COLLABORATION BY
HUNTER BELL, MICHAEL BERRESSE, SUSAN BLACKWELL, HEIDI BLICKENSTAFF, JEFF BOWEN & LARRY PRESSGROVE

WITH

HUNTER BELL   SUSAN BLACKWELL   HEIDI BLICKENSTAFF   JEFF BOWEN

SCENIC DESIGN
NEIL PATEL

COSTUME DESIGN
GREGORY GALE

LIGHTING DESIGN
JEFF CROITER & GRANT YEAGER

SOUND DESIGN
ACME SOUND PARTNERS

PROJECTION DESIGN
RICHARD DIBELLA

ORCHESTRATIONS
LARRY PRESSGROVE & ROB PREUSS

VOCAL ARRANGEMENTS
JEFF BOWEN & LARRY PRESSGROVE

MUSIC COORDINATOR
HOWARD JOINES

PRODUCTION MANAGER
DAVE NELSON

PRESS REPRESENTATIVE
SAM RUDY MEDIA RELATIONS

ASSISTANT STAGE MANAGER
TOM REYNOLDS

PRODUCTION STAGE MANAGER
MARTHA DONALDSON

MUSICAL DIRECTION
LARRY PRESSGROVE

DIRECTED AND CHOREOGRAPHED BY

MICHAEL BERRESSE

DEVELOPMENT OF *NOW. HERE. THIS.* WAS SUPPORTED BY THE EUGENE O'NEILL THEATRE CENTER DURING A RESIDENCY AT THE CABARET AND PERFORMANCE CONFERENCE OF 2009.

WE ARE GRATEFUL FOR THE ADDITIONAL DEVELOPMENT SUPPORT GIVEN TO *NOW. HERE. THIS.* BY:
WESTON PLAYHOUSE THEATRE COMPANY, THE MACDOWELL ARTISTS COLONY, OMI INTERNATIONAL ARTS CENTER, AND GOODSPEED MUSICALS.

ISBN 978-1-4803-5433-3

7777 W. BLUEMOUND RD. P.O. BOX 13819 MILWAUKEE, WI 53213

Visit Hal Leonard Online at
www.halleonard.com

Jeff Bowen (Music and Lyrics) wrote the music and lyrics for the Broadway musical *[title of show]* (OBIE award) in which he also starred. He has written music and lyrics for *Villains Tonight!* for the Walt Disney Company and the theme songs for the web series' "the [title of show] show" and "Squad '85." His songs can be heard on the original cast album of *[title of show]*, as well as *Broadway Bares Openings* and *Over the Moon: The Broadway Lullaby Project* recordings. Jeff is a proud member of ASCAP, AEA, Writers Guild, Dramatists Guild, and the National Audubon Society. Twitter: @jefbowen

Hunter Bell (Book) earned an OBIE Award, a Drama League nomination, and a Tony nomination for Best Book of a Musical for the Broadway musical *[title of show]*. Other credits include books for *Silence! The Musical, Bellobration!* (Ringling Bros. Circus), *Villains Tonight!* (Disney Cruise Lines), *Found, Other World,* and Julie Andrews' *The Great American Mousical.* He is a co-creator of the web series "the [title of show] show" and has developed television with ABC Studios. Hunter is a proud graduate and distinguished alumnus of Webster University's Conservatory of Theatre Arts, a member of the Dramatists Guild, Writers Guild, and a MacDowell Fellow. Twitter: @huntbell

Susan Blackwell (Book) is on a mission to free people's self-expression. She champions this cause as a performer, writer, educator and business consultant. She played a character based on herself in the original Broadway musical *[title of show],* and the off-Broadway musical *Now. Here. This.* She created and hosts the freewheeling chat show "Side by Side by Susan Blackwell" on Broadway.com. As the founder of Susan Blackwell & Co, she partners with like-minded, compassionate artists and thought leaders to deliver inspiring entertainment and educational offerings aimed at freeing people's creativity and self-expression. www.susanblackwell.com Twitter: @Susan_Blackwell

WHAT ARE THE ODDS?

Music and Lyrics by
JEFF BOWEN

Allegro

SUSAN:
Four point fif-ty sev-en bil-lion years a-go a

ti-ny speck ap-pears out in space. ___ In the black sits a qui-et-ly

spin-ning sphere ___ where some-thing wack is a-bout to take place. ___

new and bi - zarre one _____ is a - bout to be -

Moderately fast Rock

gin. _____

HUNTER:

Her - mit crabs and ba - by tur - tles start

crawl- lin' 'round ev - 'ry - where _____ and be - fore we know _ it, there are

HUNTER:
Years whiz by like Bo - die Mil - ler ski - ing. The

earth is run - ning ram - pant with the hu - man be - ing. _____ And

ALL:

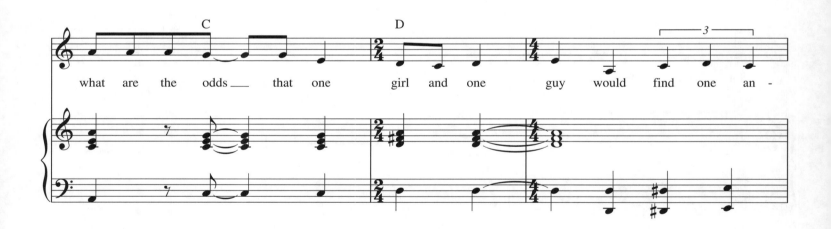

C   D
what are the odds ___ that one girl and one guy would find one an -

Fmaj7   E7   Am
oth - er and u - ni - fy?

HUNTER & JEFF:
A

MORE LIFE

Music and Lyrics by
JEFF BOWEN

So man-y hours __ are spent __ want-ing some-thing and all ____ that it does __ is just

SUSAN & HEIDI:
flood me with ques - tions _____ like: Where __ will I find it?

HUNTER & JEFF:
flood me with ques - tions _____ like: Where will I

What __ will it feel like? _____ And

find it? What will it feel like? _____

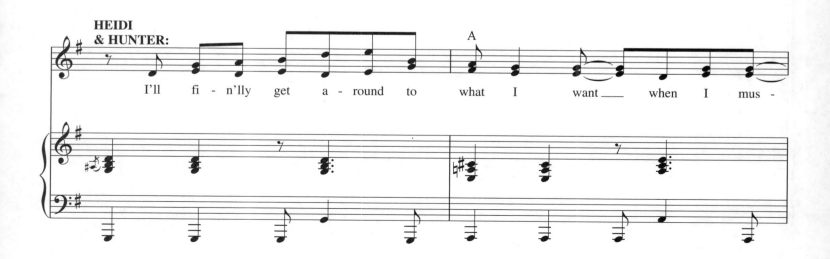

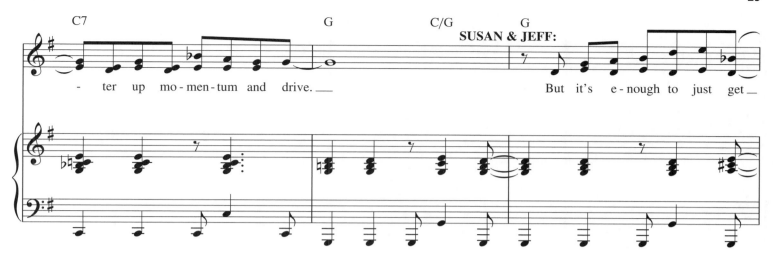

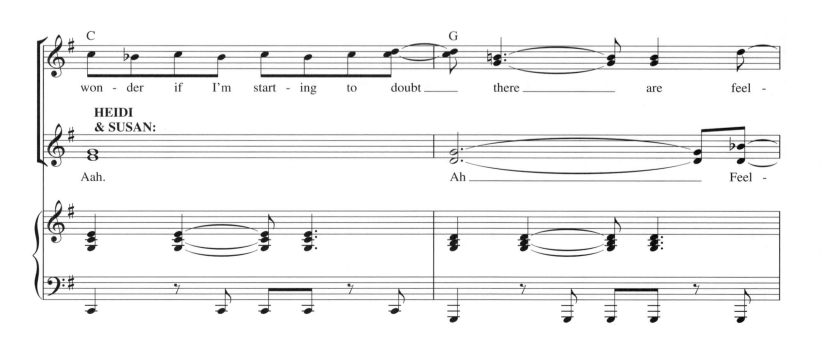

_____ and has a tren - dy name _ like Max _ or Mis - ter Win - ston Spar - kles.

HUNTER:
I want to be de - sir - - ed. _____

like All - Star Com - ics num - ber eight! _ I

I want a pair of jeans _ that make _ me look awe - some. _

I want less re - spon - si - bil - i - ty.

I want a pair of jeans _ that make _ me look awe - some. _ I want whit - er teeth _ and I

want e - nough mon - ey so I _____ can re - tire _____ and tra -

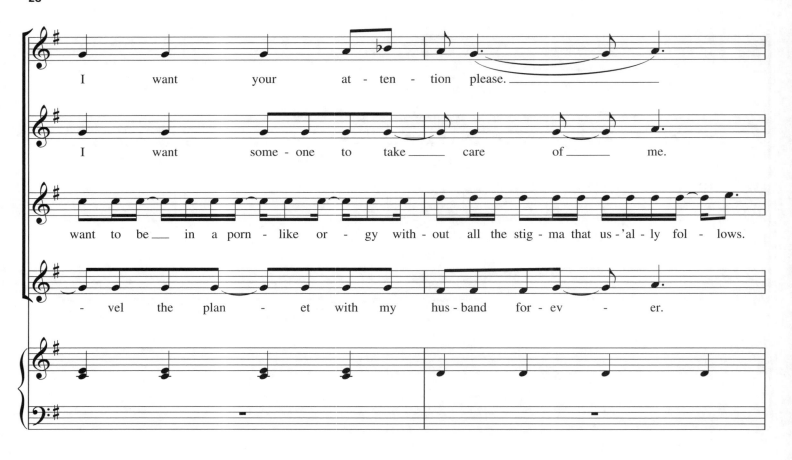

I want your at - ten - tion please. _____

I want some - one to take ____ care of ____ me.

want to be ___ in a porn - like or - gy with - out all the stig - ma that us - 'al - ly fol - lows.

- vel the plan - et with my hus - band for - ev - er.

Em

I wan-na be - lieve ____ I'm con - fi - dent _ suc - cess - ful, want - ed and

I want to feel pret - ty. I want to be con - fi - dent, _ suc - cess - ful, want - ed and

I want to leave ____ it all ____ and rise ____ a - bove. ____

D

I want to take leave ____ to the South Pa - cif - ic to see the So -

DAZZLE CAMOUFLAGE

Music and Lyrics by
JEFF BOWEN

Allegro animato

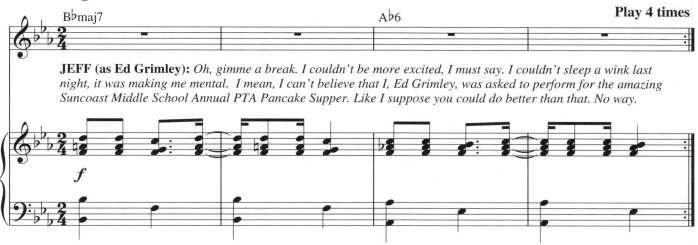

JEFF (as Ed Grimley): *Oh, gimme a break. I couldn't be more excited, I must say. I couldn't sleep a wink last night, it was making me mental. I mean, I can't believe that I, Ed Grimley, was asked to perform for the amazing Suncoast Middle School Annual PTA Pancake Supper. Like I suppose you could do better than that. No way.*

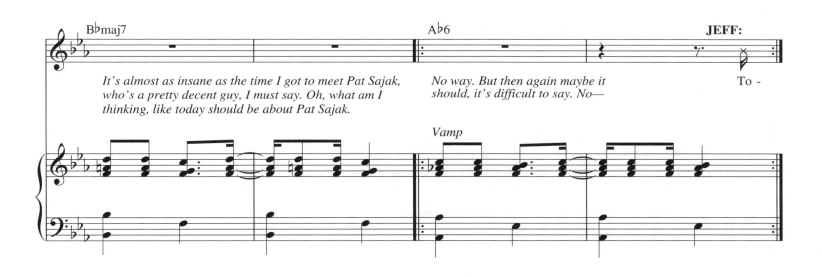

It's almost as insane as the time I got to meet Pat Sajak, who's a pretty decent guy, I must say. Oh, what am I thinking, like today should be about Pat Sajak.

No way. But then again maybe it should, it's difficult to say. No—

JEFF:

To -

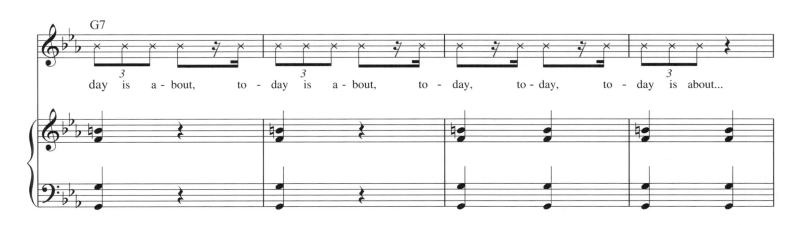

day is a-bout, to-day is a-bout, to-day, to-day, to-day is about...

32

A - maze - ment he en - joys.

JEFF: *You know what moose knuckle is, don't you?*

Cam - el toe for

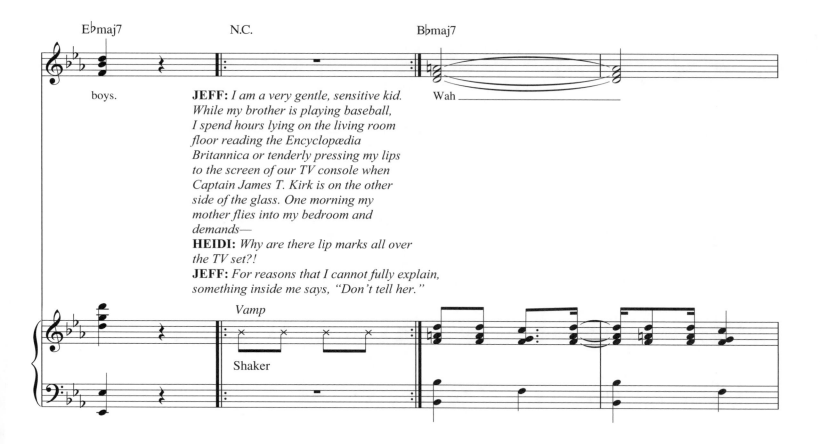

boys.

JEFF: *I am a very gentle, sensitive kid. While my brother is playing baseball, I spend hours lying on the living room floor reading the Encyclopædia Britannica or tenderly pressing my lips to the screen of our TV console when Captain James T. Kirk is on the other side of the glass. One morning my mother flies into my bedroom and demands—*
HEIDI: *Why are there lip marks all over the TV set?!*
JEFF: *For reasons that I cannot fully explain, something inside me says, "Don't tell her."*

Wah

Vamp

Shaker

34

This dazzle camouflage confused the enemy's rangefinders. Huge boats could hide in plain sight and bomber planes would just pass them by.

JEFF: *A light bulb goes off! If I could dazzle everyone around me, I could hide in plain sight. Then maybe I would hear Shane Fessler say:*
HUNTER: *Dude, you're funny!*
JEFF: *Instead of:*
HUNTER: *Dude, you're a faggot!*

JEFF: *So I tuck away Quiet Me, Sensitive Me. And I become... Dazzle Me!*

And I have a million different cards in my Razzle Dazzle deck.

JEFF (as Dumb Jock Teacher): *Look at me! I teach Driver's Ed!*

38

GIVE ME YOUR ATTENTION

Music and Lyrics by
JEFF BOWEN

Funky Pop

HEIDI:
Christ-mas din-ner is done, it's

time for a show on the liv-ing room floor. I make my cous-in Al-li-son__ sing

"Mich-ael Row the Boat__ A-shore"__ and then I make my cou-sin Rod-dy play

G♭maj7

phone rings and then my heart stops right in mid scrub. She

E♭m6 · · · B♭m · · · · **SUSAN:**

leaves the bath-room for a mo-ment then comes back. Did you

colla voce *a tempo*

F♭(♭5) N.C. **SUSAN:**

leave Mis-sus Thor-ton's house to-day? __ **HEIDI:** *No.* Did you

F♭(♭5) N.C. **HEIDI:**

pour bleach and salt on her kitch-en floor? **HEIDI:** *No.* Then she

shakes her head and she leaves me a-lone in the tub and though the

shamp-oo's drip-pin' down __ and it burns, I should men - tion that it

real - ly does-n't mat-ter 'cause at least I got her __ at - ten - tion. _____ I

Tempo I

want more op-pur-tu-ni-ties to stand out from the crowd. Give me your at-ten-tion please, I

ARCHER

Music and Lyrics by
JEFF BOWEN

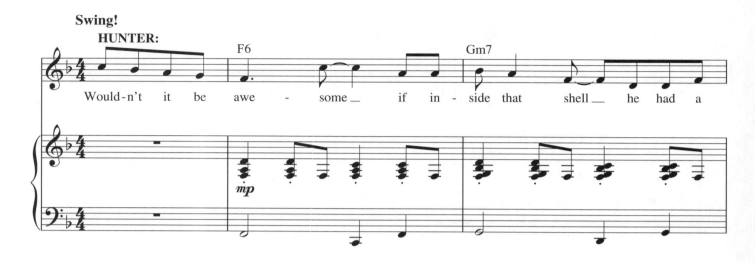

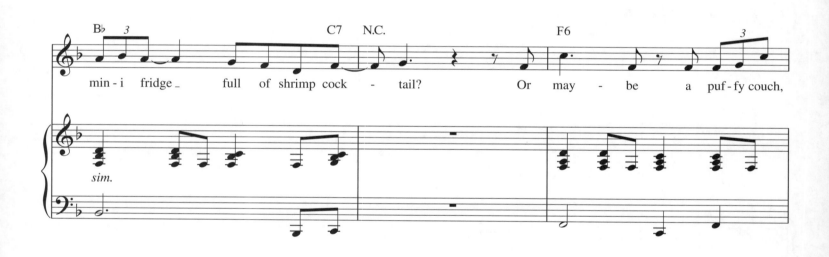

56

MEMBERS ONLY

Music and Lyrics by
JEFF BOWEN

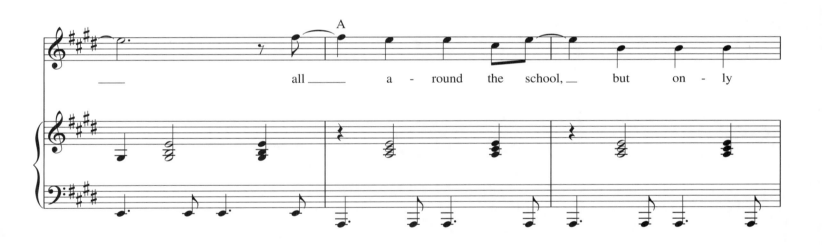

60

off I-zod shirt! D'you know what this means? __ I got my

ti - cket, __ now I'm im-pos-si-ble to ig - nore. __

__ This guar-an - tees the trus-tees hand me the keys __ that

o - pen up that door. __

JEFF: Hey, Tan-ya.

HEIDI: Hey, Jeff.

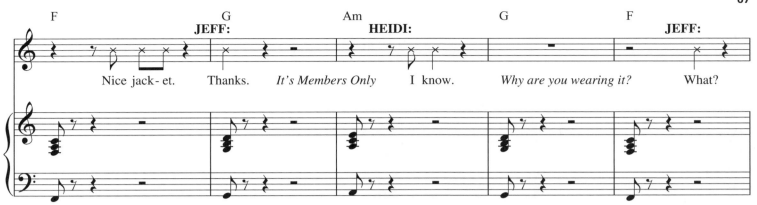

Nice jack-et. | Thanks. | *It's Members Only* | I know. | *Why are you wearing it?* | What?

I don't know. | **HEIDI:** *You do realize that this is Southwest Florida and it's like a thousand degrees out, right?* | Yeah.

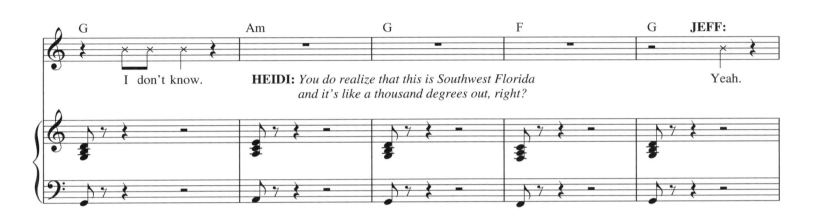

What's that smell? | I don't know. | Gross. | *If you're gonna wear that jacket, at least wear deodorant, too.* | Hey, Vic-ki.

Hey, Sus-san. | That's a cute top. | Where'd you get it? | Oh, this? | Um... | I don't

know... um...   Par - is?   Cool.   *I think they make these jeans in France, too.*   Oh.

Are those Gloria Vanderbilts?   These?   Yeah, I think so.   They look good on you.

Thanks. Yours do, too.   **HEIDI:** *Oh, these are Guess jeans. I don't really wear GVs anymore. I don't even know where mine are.*   Hey, Bet- sy.   Hey... *I don't remember your name.*

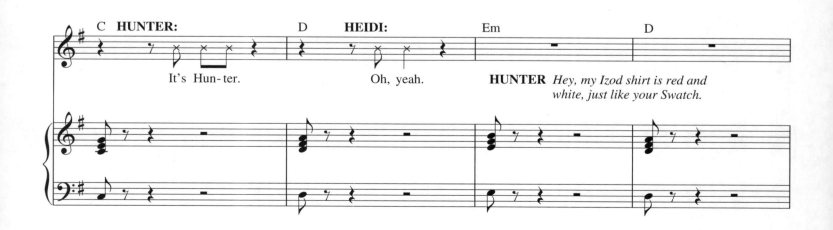

It's Hun- ter.   Oh, yeah.   **HUNTER** *Hey, my Izod shirt is red and white, just like your Swatch.*

THAT'LL NEVER BE ME

Music and Lyrics by
JEFF BOWEN

prestigious university with a very fancy law school. I don't want to drop any names. Let's just say it rhymes with "Duke."

SUSAN: How'd they get ___ there? Where's that road _____ that could

HEIDI: I ___ will get ___ there. On ___ that road, ____

lead me out ___ of this no - where town ___ to - night? _____ But

lead me out ___ of this no - where town ___ to - night.

gold - en tick - ets don't ___ get mailed ___ to this one-horse town ___ zip code ___ so there

KICK ME

Music and Lyrics by
JEFF BOWEN

84

THEN COMES YOU

Music and Lyrics by
JEFF BOWEN

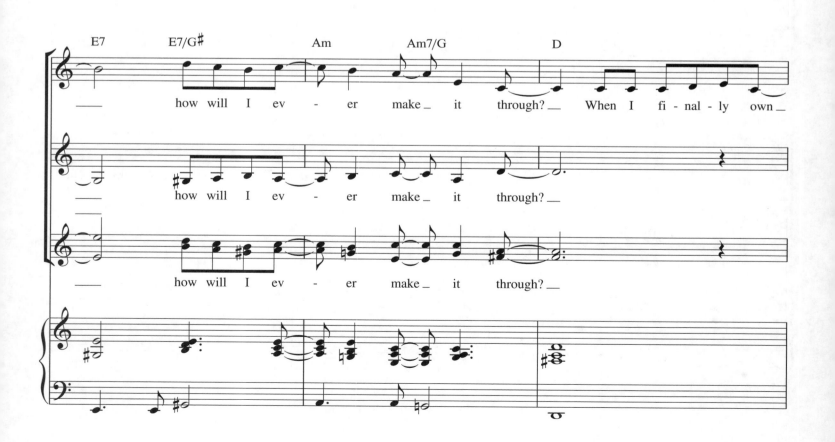

GOLDEN PALACE

Music and Lyrics by
JEFF BOWEN

HEIDI: *The.*
HUNTER: *Subject.*
JEFF: *Is.*
HEIDI: *Reading.*

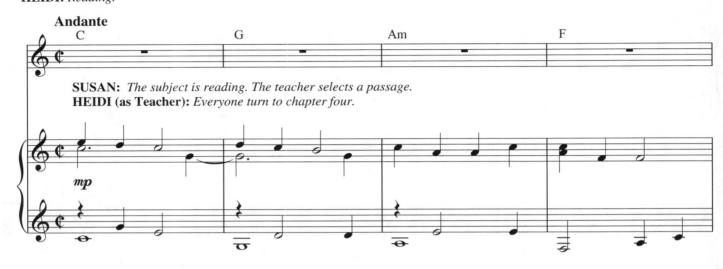

SUSAN: *The subject is reading. The teacher selects a passage.*
HEIDI (as Teacher): *Everyone turn to chapter four.*

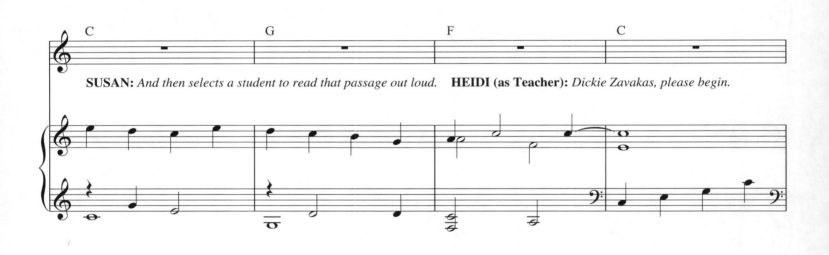

SUSAN: *And then selects a student to read that passage out loud.*   **HEIDI (as Teacher):** *Dickie Zavakas, please begin.*

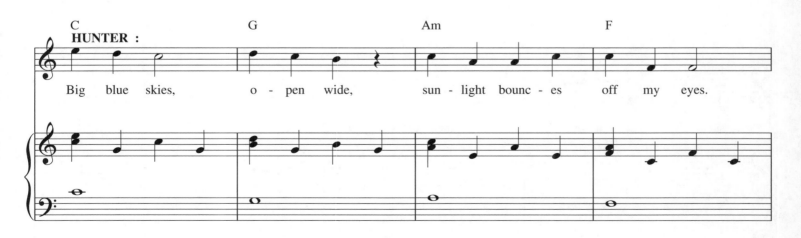

HUNTER :

Big blue skies, o - pen wide, sun - light bounc - es off my eyes.

If I shut them tight the light still gets through. ___

SUSAN: *And then the next student repeats the passage.*

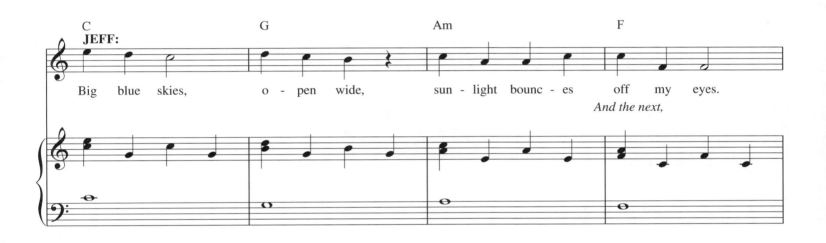

JEFF:

Big blue skies, o - pen wide, sun - light bounc - es off my eyes.

And the next,

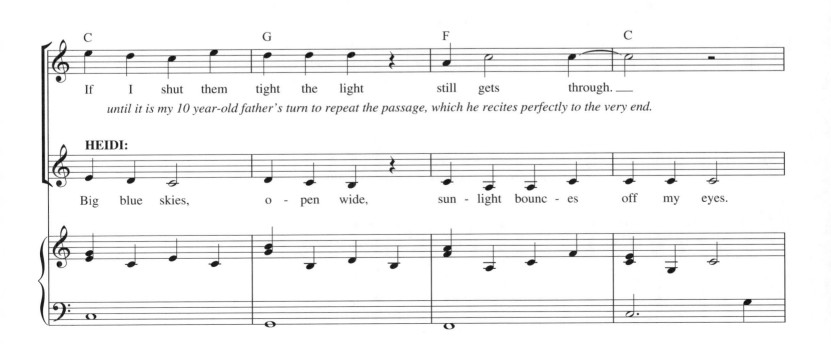

If I shut them tight the light still gets through. ___

until it is my 10 year-old father's turn to repeat the passage, which he recites perfectly to the very end.

HEIDI:

Big blue skies, o - pen wide, sun - light bounc - es off my eyes.

SUSAN:

Big blue skies, o - pen wide, sun - light bounc - es off my eyes.

If I shut them tight the light still gets through. ___

If I shut them tight the light still gets through. ___

SUSAN: *It's a warm night. My father is playing under the streetlamp with the other boys from Fairview Avenue.*

espr.

One by one, the others get called in for supper. My father lets himself into his house.

97

SUSAN: *Until one day he feels a hand touch his shoulder.*   **JEFF:** *"I can't."*
HEIDI: *Please begin.*
SUSAN: *Everybody is waiting for him to read.*
     And he has to say, in front of everyone—

SUSAN: *My father is working second shift at the GM plant. He finishes the bologna sandwiches that my mom made for him*

and solves the last squares of the crossword puzzle. He still has some time before he has to return to the factory floor.

He fishes an old unemployment check stub out of the pocket of his coveralls, takes his Bic pen and begins to write a poem,

like Tom in The Glass Menagerie *in the warehouse writing on the back of a shoe box.*

HUNTER & JEFF:
There in - side ___ are nov - el - ists ___ and fine mu - si - cians

HEIDI:
build - ing great works of art. ___

SUSAN: *I'm home from school on winter break. Speaking of, my dad's in school, too, now. How 'bout that?*
JEFF (as Dad): *We're both gonna get our Masters at the same time.*

SUSAN: *I'm organizing some boxes and papers, and I find the old check stub with a poem written* **JEFF:** *Naw, now. I can't.*
on the back in his handwriting. "Dad, this is good! You can really write!"

SUSAN: *The Golden Palace is where the Beautiful People and the Great Thinkers of this and previous*
generations convene to bask in each others brilliance and create all the great works of art. It's
all going down in the Golden Palace.

HUNTER: *Michelangelo's David.* **HEIDI:** To Kill A Mockingbird. **JEFF:** *The X-Men.*
SUSAN: *Yes. Great work. Worthy work. And the people that populate that place and pump out those important*
paintings and poems and pieces are deeply intelligent, stunning, clean, privileged people.

There's no room in the Golden Palace for girls like me. Girls who
come from what I come from.

Slowly, tranquil

N.C.

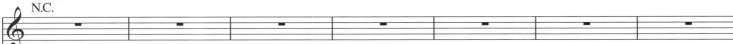

SUSAN: *I see my hands resting on the keyboard of my laptop. I look past my hands and the keyboard and I see through
the panes of my studio window out into the sharp winter woods. I am typing this sentence at The MacDowell
Artists Colony in Peterborough, New Hampshire, where I have been granted a residency to work alongside
some of the greatest artists and writers on the planet; to write the words you are listening to right now. It hits me.*

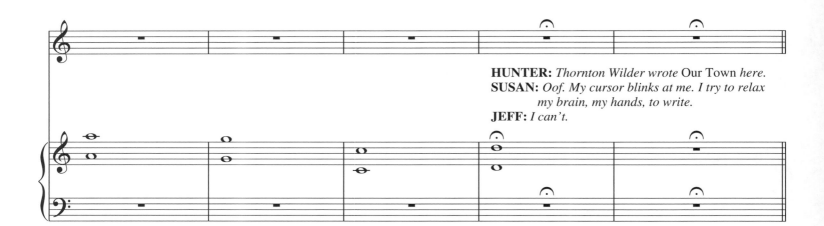

HUNTER: *Thornton Wilder wrote* Our Town *here.*
SUSAN: *Oof. My cursor blinks at me. I try to relax
my brain, my hands, to write.*
JEFF: *I can't.*

Tempo I

Am   G   F

SUSAN: *I check to see if cell phone coverage is squeaking its way through the New Hampshire woods and into my studio.
On my Facebook news feed, someone updates their status with this quote from John Adams to his wife Abigail:*

Am   G   F6/9

Play 4 times

HUNTER: *"May 12, 1780. I must study politics and war that my sons may have liberty to study mathematics and philosophy.*
HEIDI: *Everybody is waiting for him to read*
HUNTER: *"My sons ought to study mathematics and philosophy, geography, natural history, naval architecture—"*
JEFF: *We're both gonna get our Masters at the same time.*
HUNTER: *"In order to give their children a right to study music, painting, poetry.*

SUSAN: *I have been granted a residency at The MacDowell Artists Colony. I feel a hand touch my shoulder.*
HEIDI: *Please begin.*
HUNTER: *Please begin.*
JEFF: *Please begin.*
SUSAN: *There is a Golden Palace. It's a Chinese restaurant located at 321 Nashua Street in Milford, New Hampshire.*

SUSAN: *It's not over the horizon. It's not out of reach.*

The Golden Palace is anywhere we make it. It's anywhere we make anything we want to make. And there's room for all of us:

Illiterate boys. The poets they become. Awkward girls with big faces and big feet and strange ideas. We all belong here.

My fingers begin to move, to pluck letters, to arrange them in order.
HEIDI: *The.*
HUNTER: *Subject.*
JEFF: *Is.*
HEIDI: *Reading.*

THIS TIME

Music and Lyrics by
JEFF BOWEN